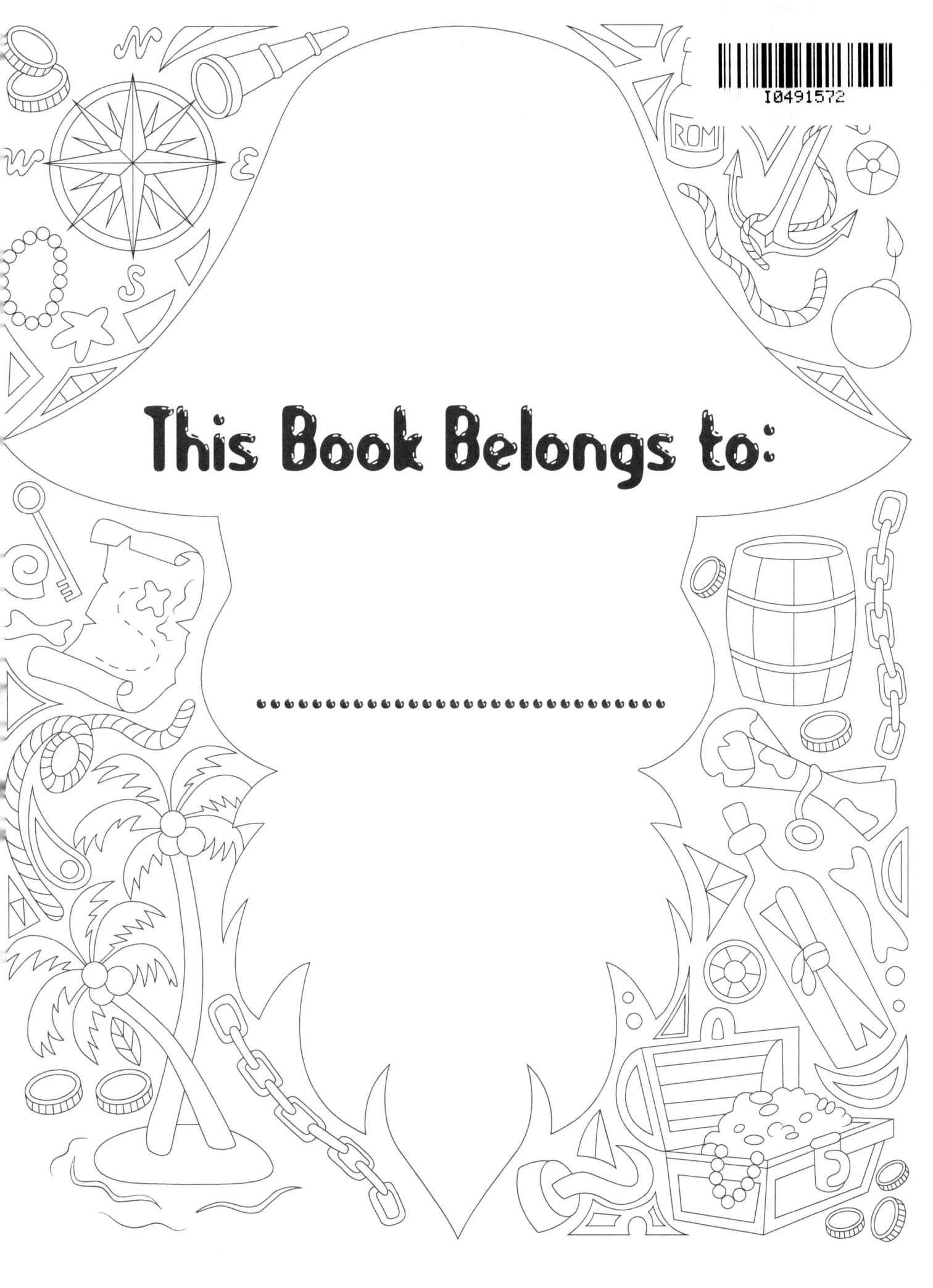

This Book Belongs to:

· ·

I0491572

Are you looking for unique **SUGAR SKULL** designs to **COLOR**? This book contains **20** totally different **HAND-DRAWN** Sugar Skull **CHARACTERS**. Each of them has a **THEMATIC BACKGROUND** with many details to color. You will love them!

Every picture is printed on **ONE SIDE** of a paper for easy removal. You can put it to the **LETTER-SIZE** frame to show your **ARTISTIC WORK**. For coloring you can use your favorite pens, pencils and markers. If you use markers we recommend to place a peace of paper behind the coloring page for non-bleeding through.

Feel free to **SHARE** pictures with your art-works and to **WRITE** your review on **AMAZON, FACEBOOK, TWITTER**.

Have **FUN** and **ENJOY COLORING!**

E-mail: SunlifeDrawing@gmail.com
Twitter: @SunlifeDrawing
Amazon Author's Page: Amazon.com/author/sunlifedrawing

LIST OF SUGAR SKULL CHARACTERS:

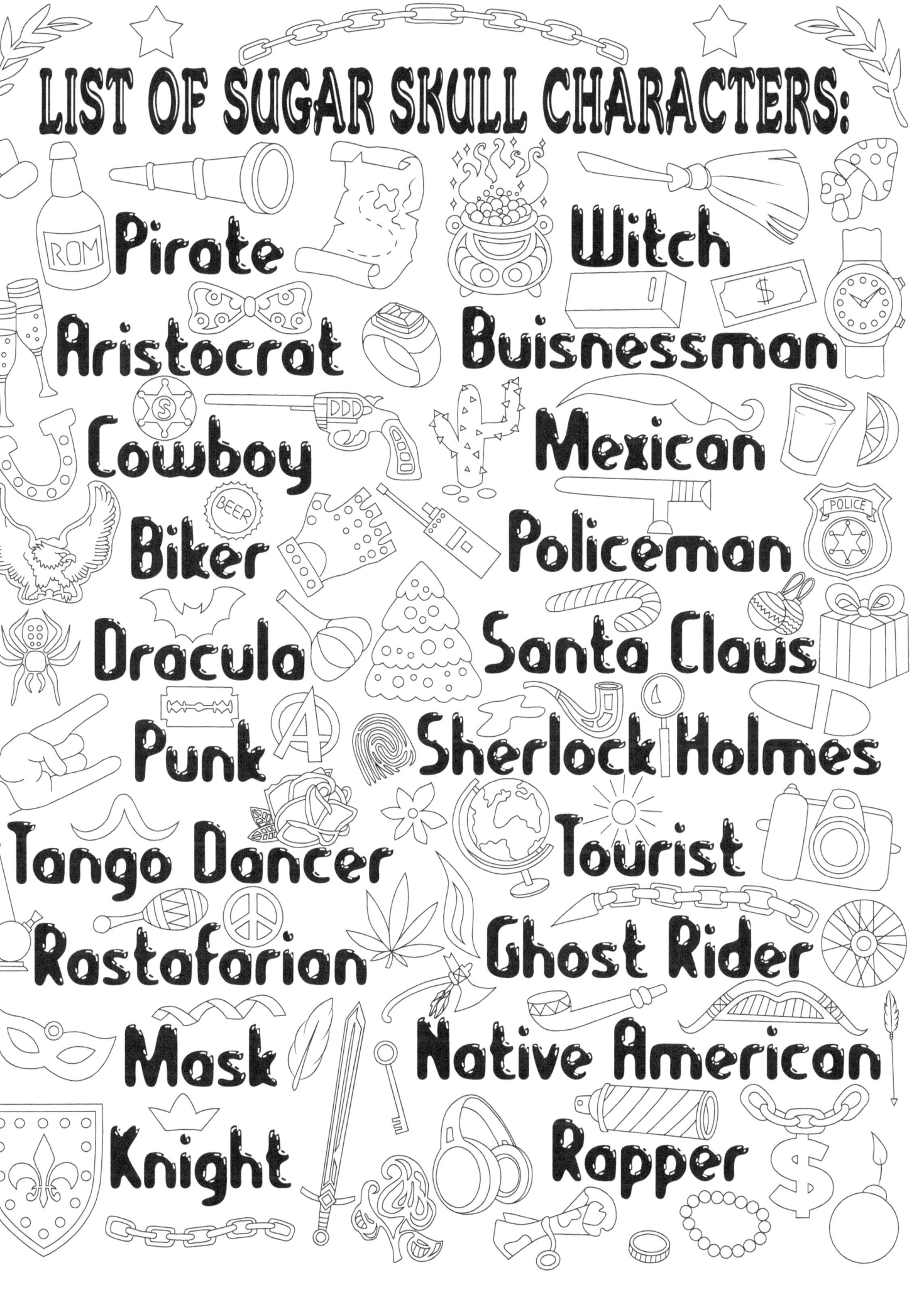

- Pirate
- Aristocrat
- Cowboy
- Biker
- Dracula
- Punk
- Tango Dancer
- Rastafarian
- Mask
- Knight
- Witch
- Buisnessman
- Mexican
- Policeman
- Santa Claus
- Sherlock Holmes
- Tourist
- Ghost Rider
- Native American
- Rapper

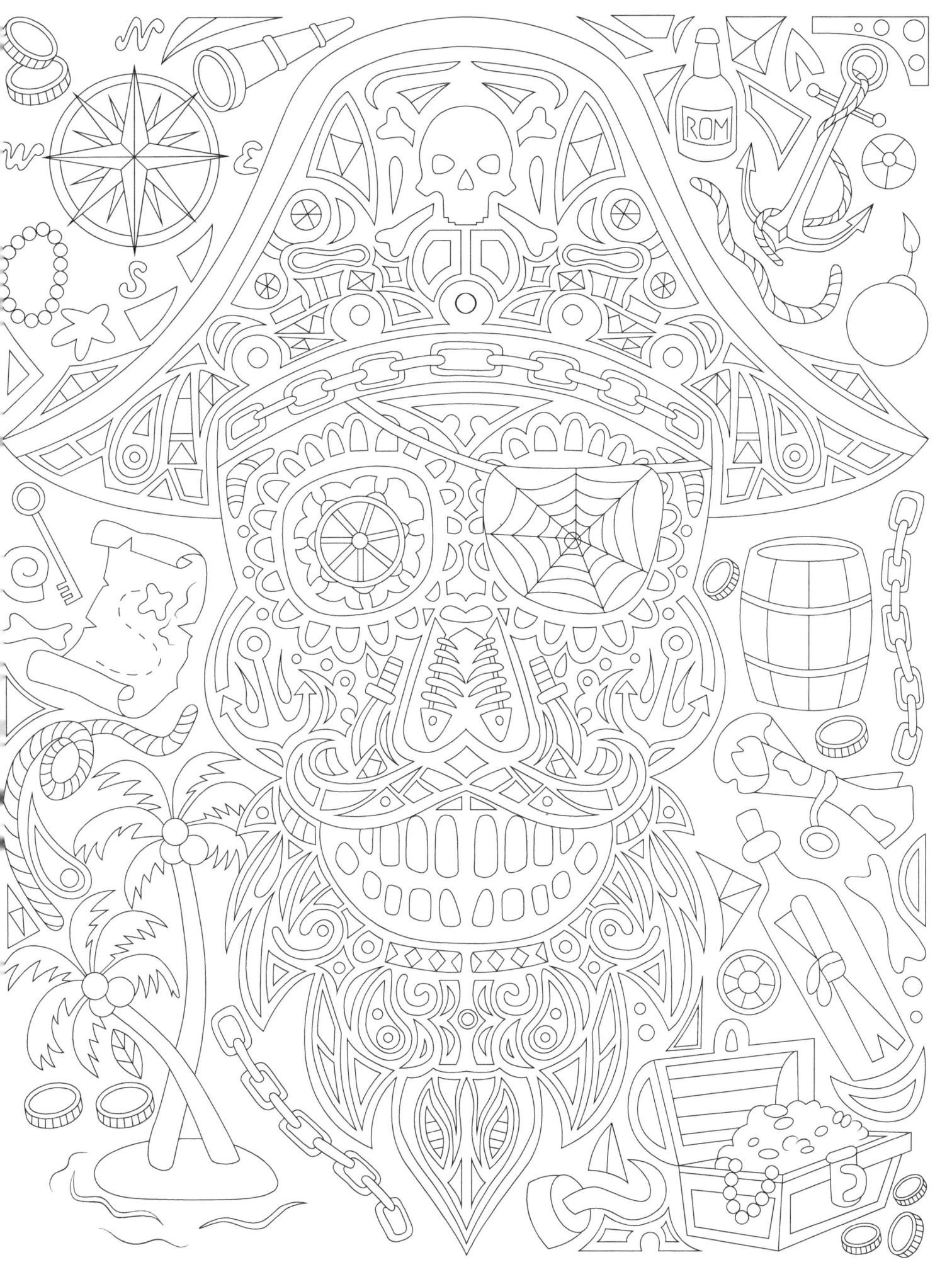

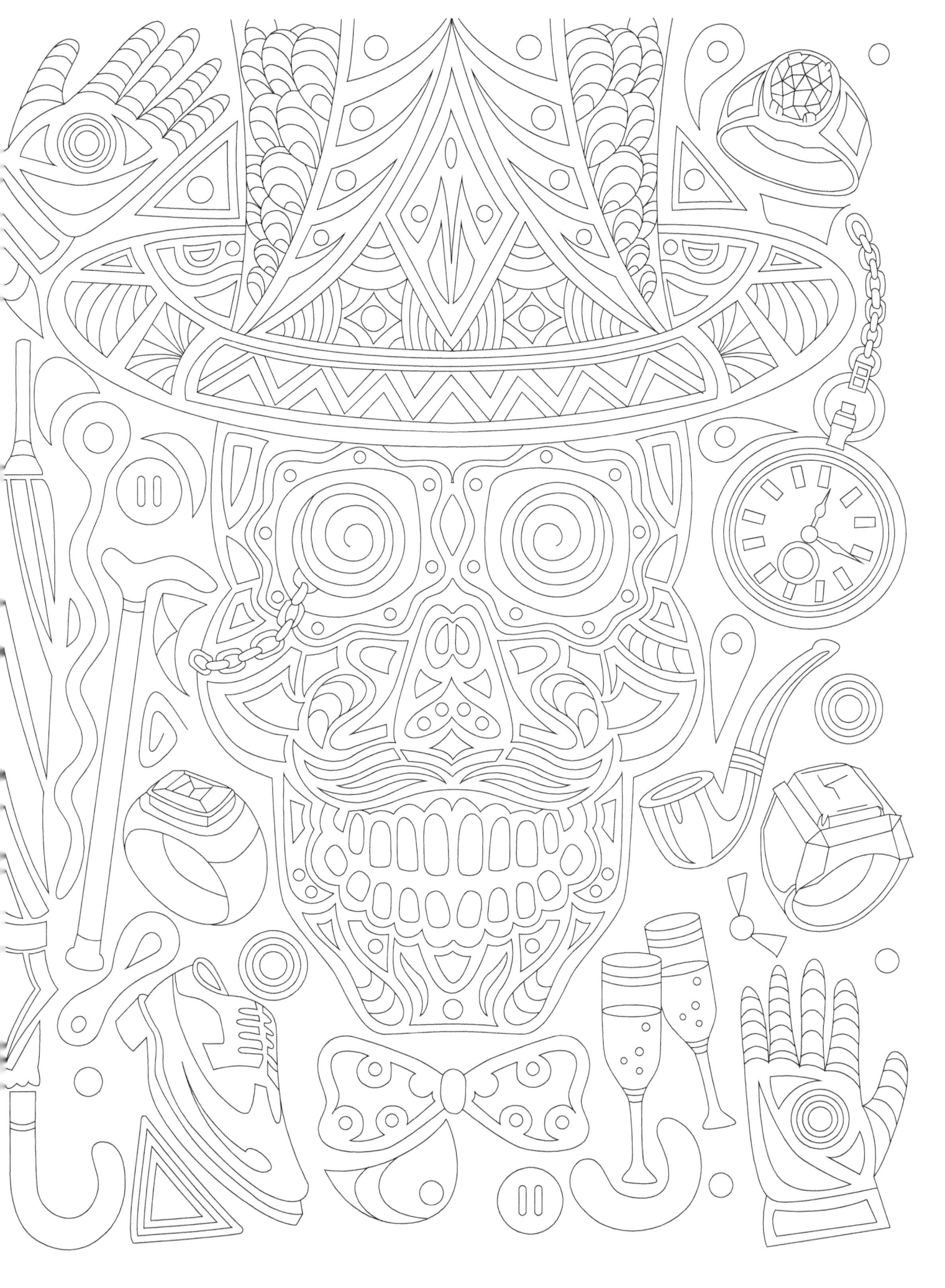

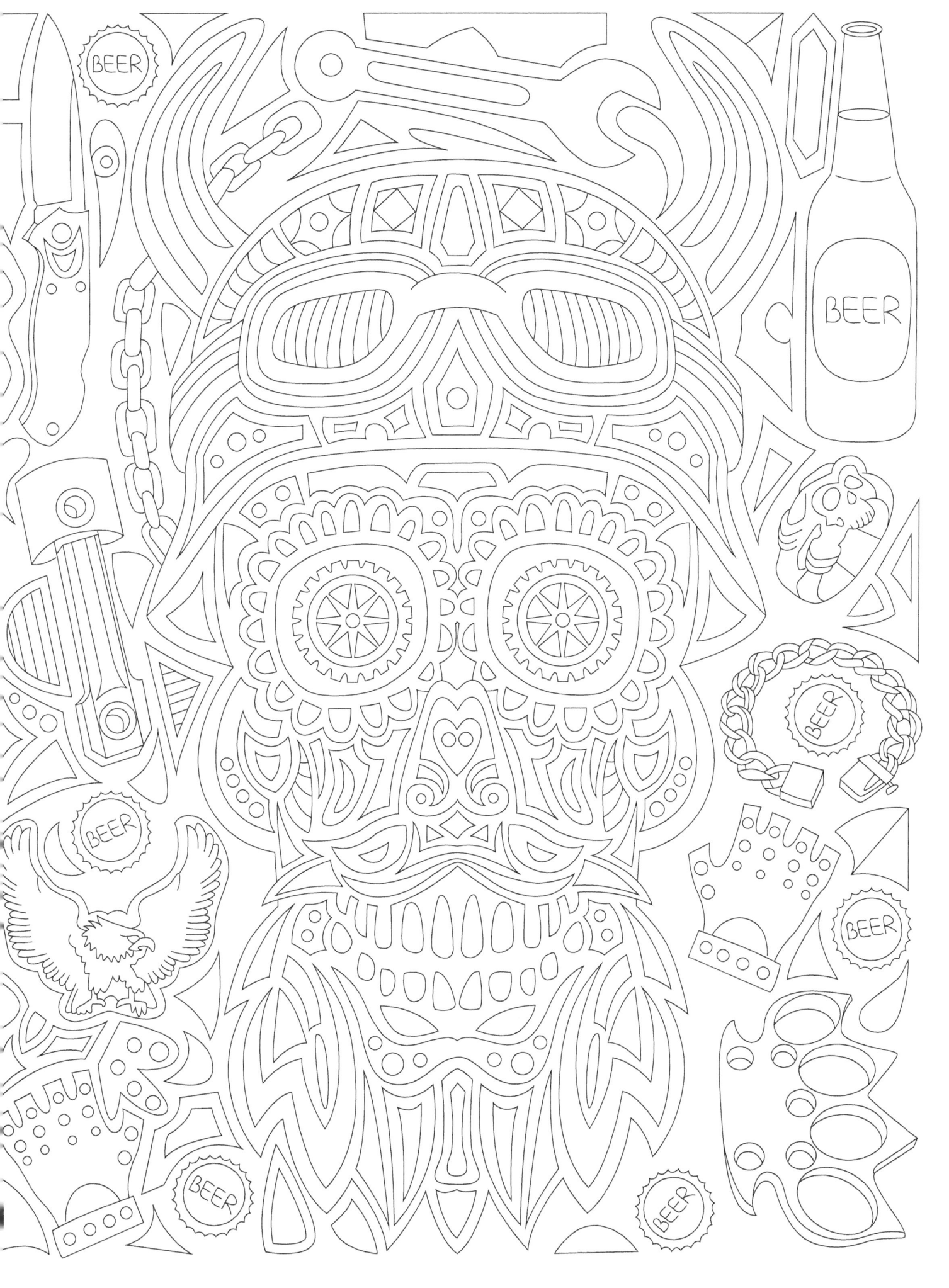

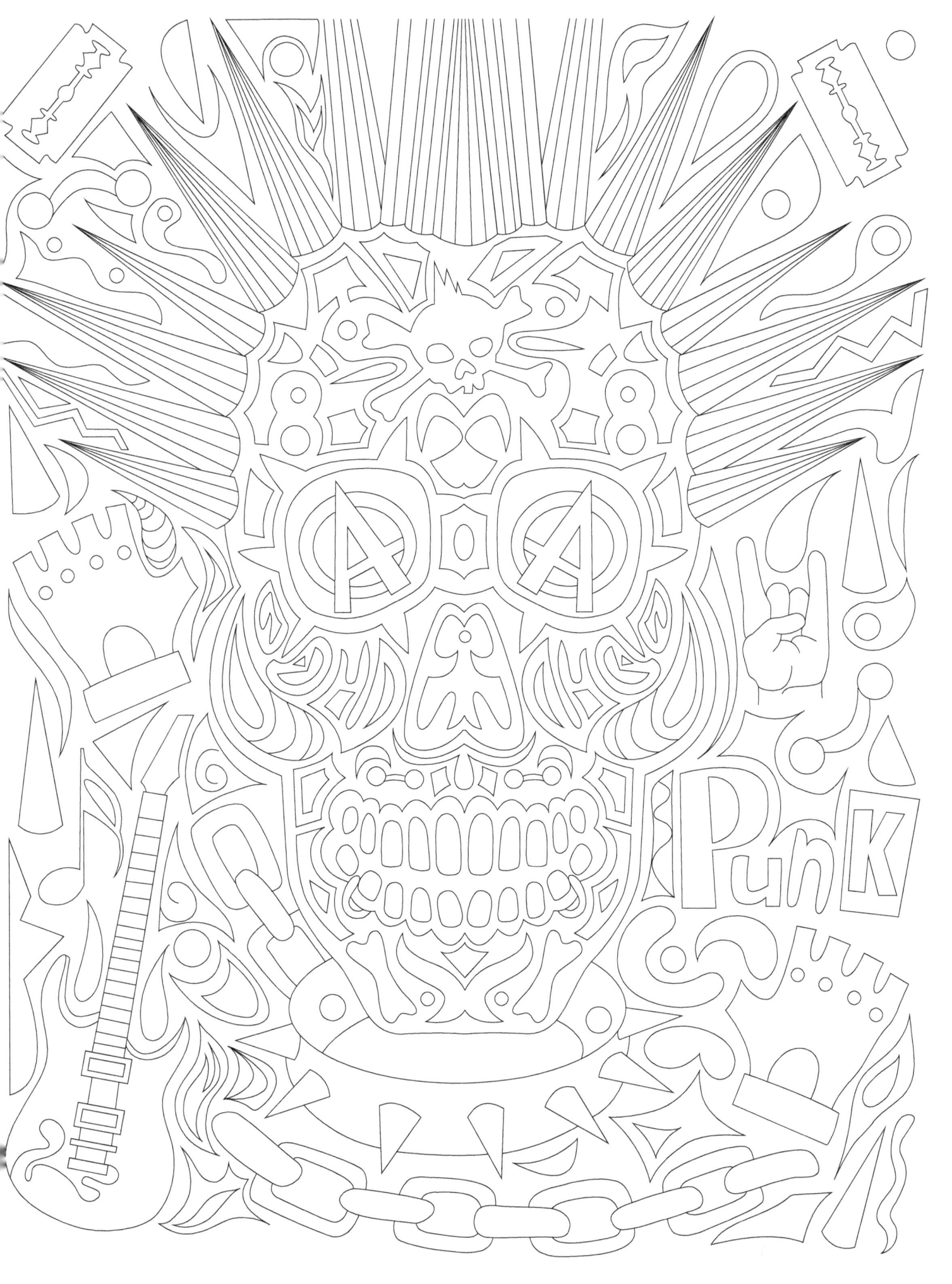

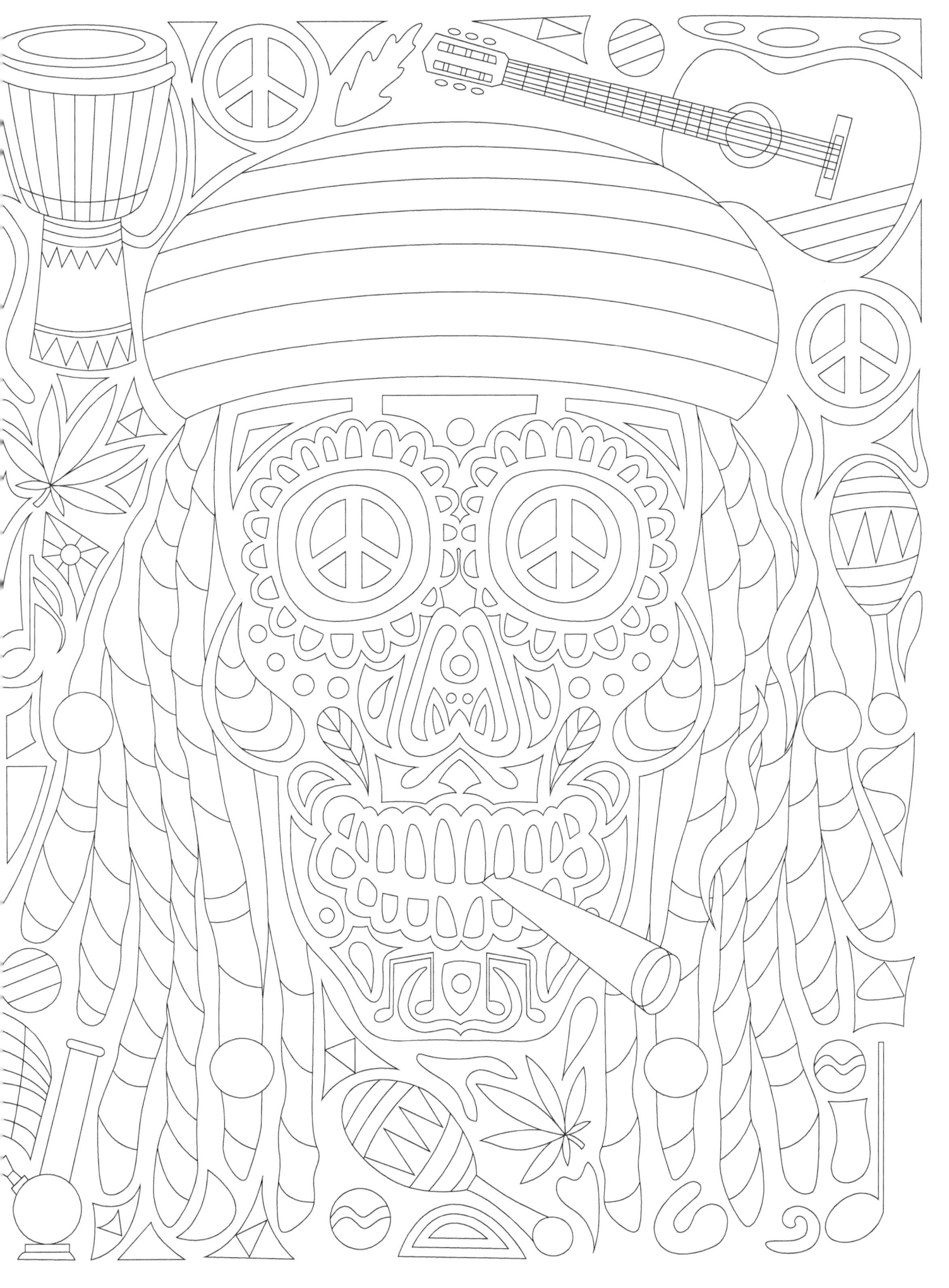

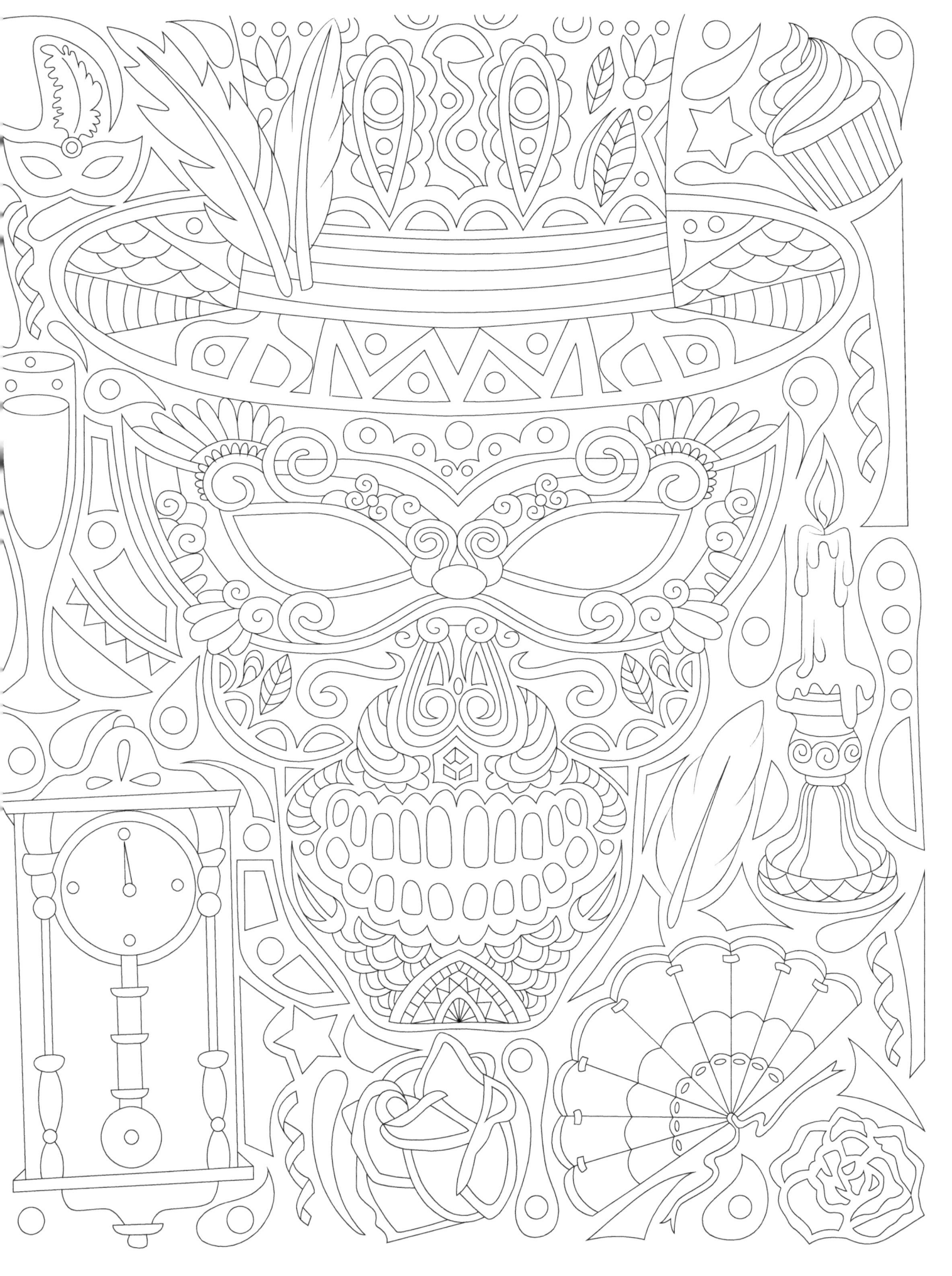

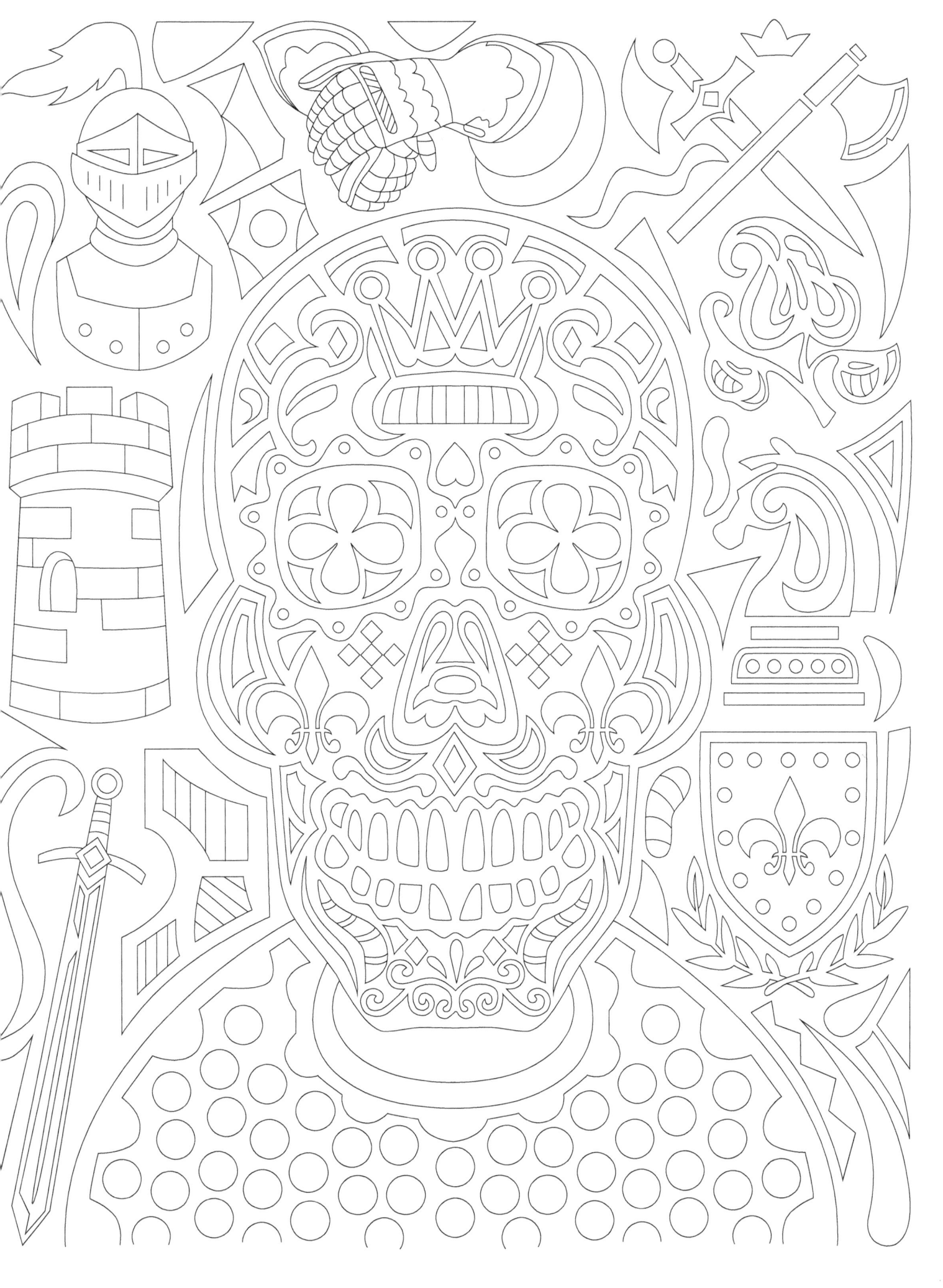

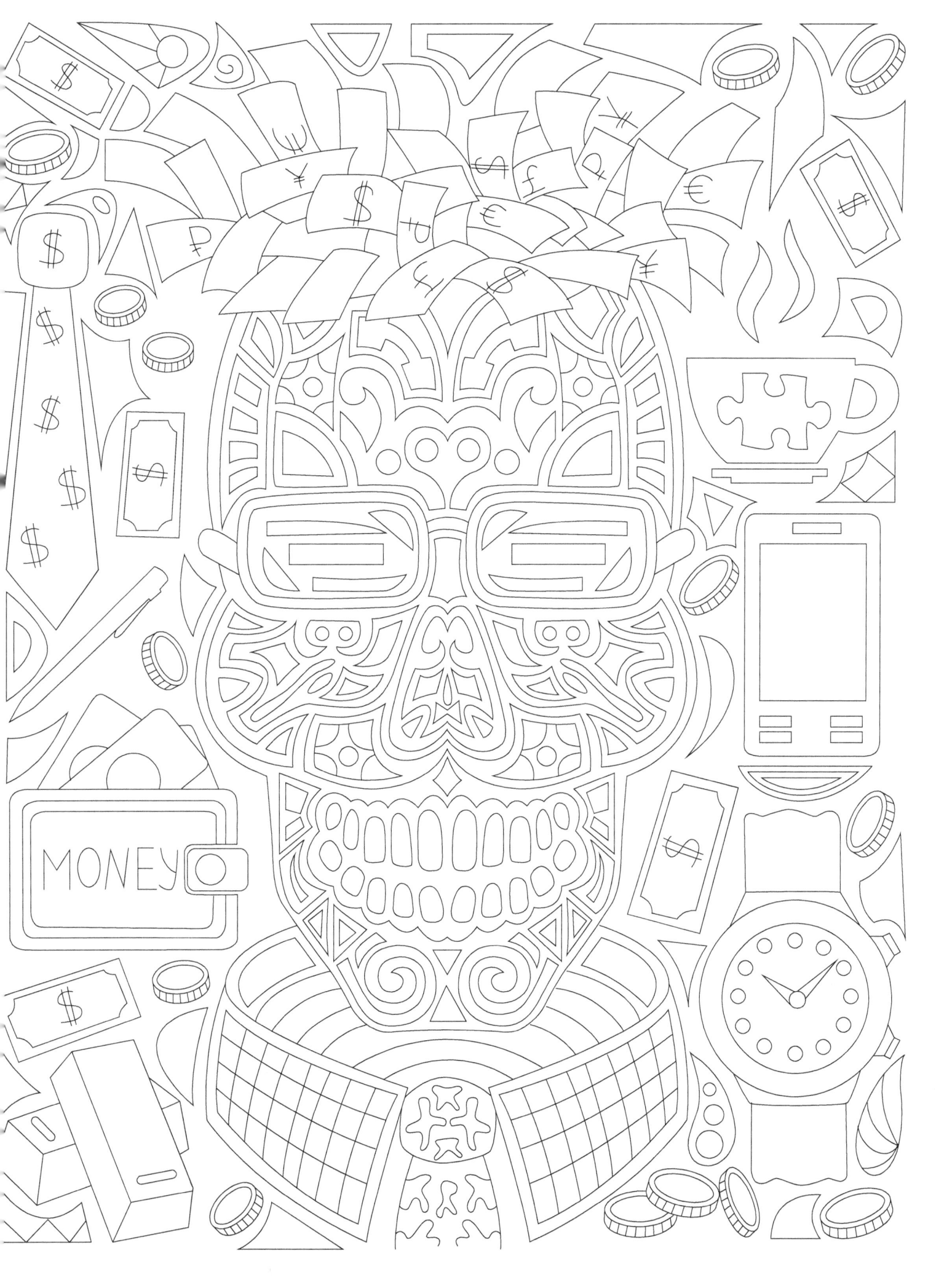

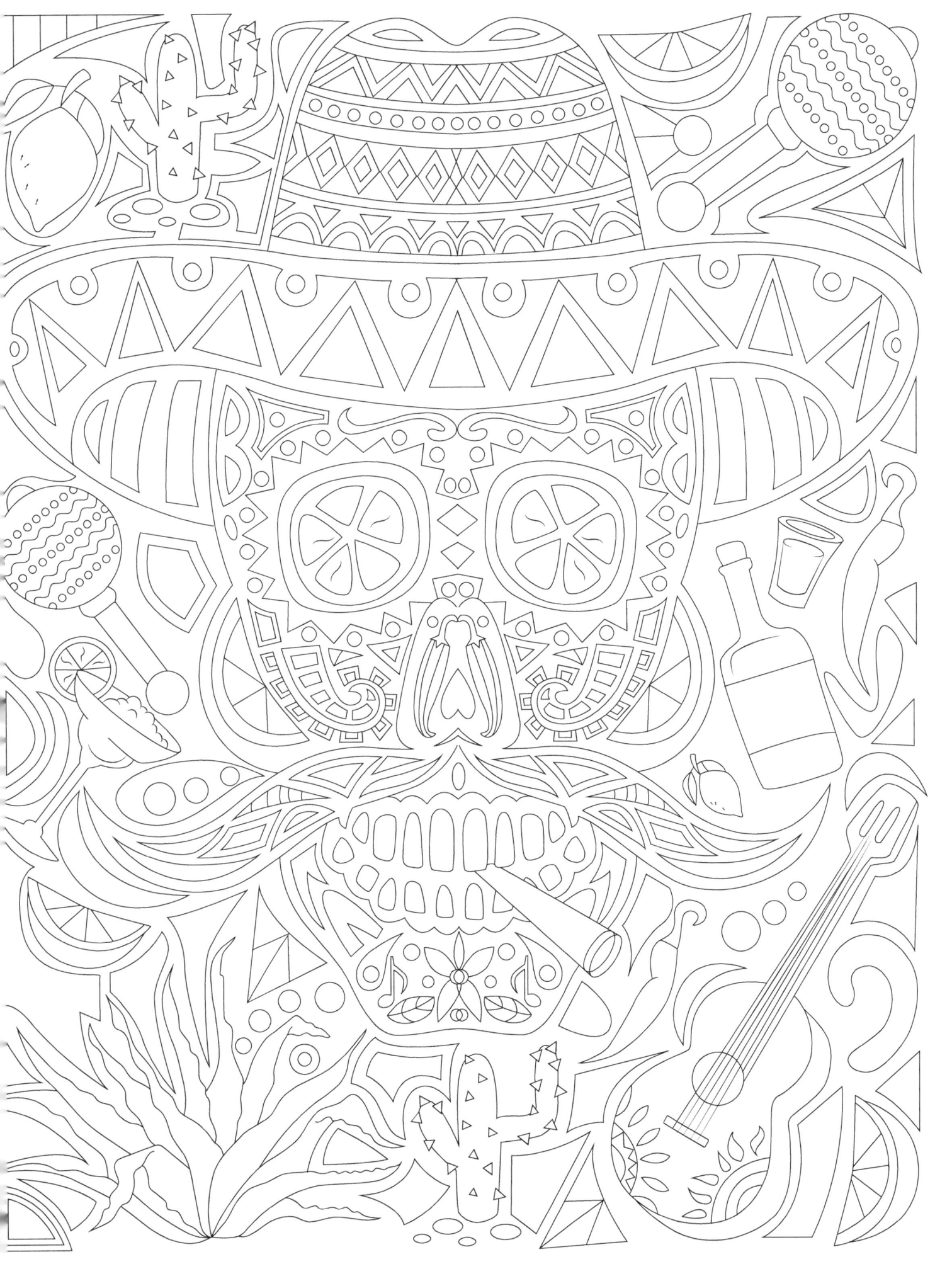

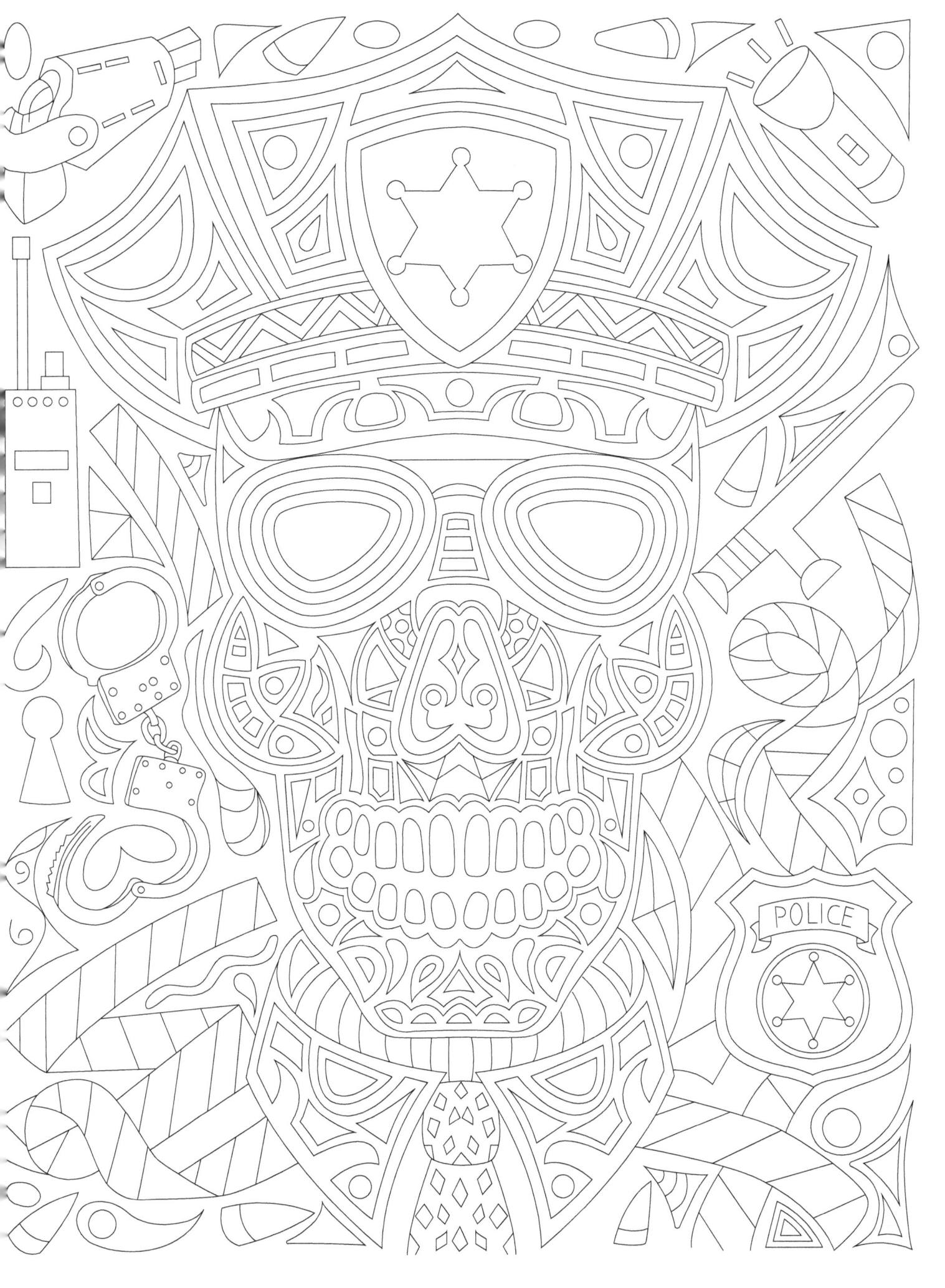

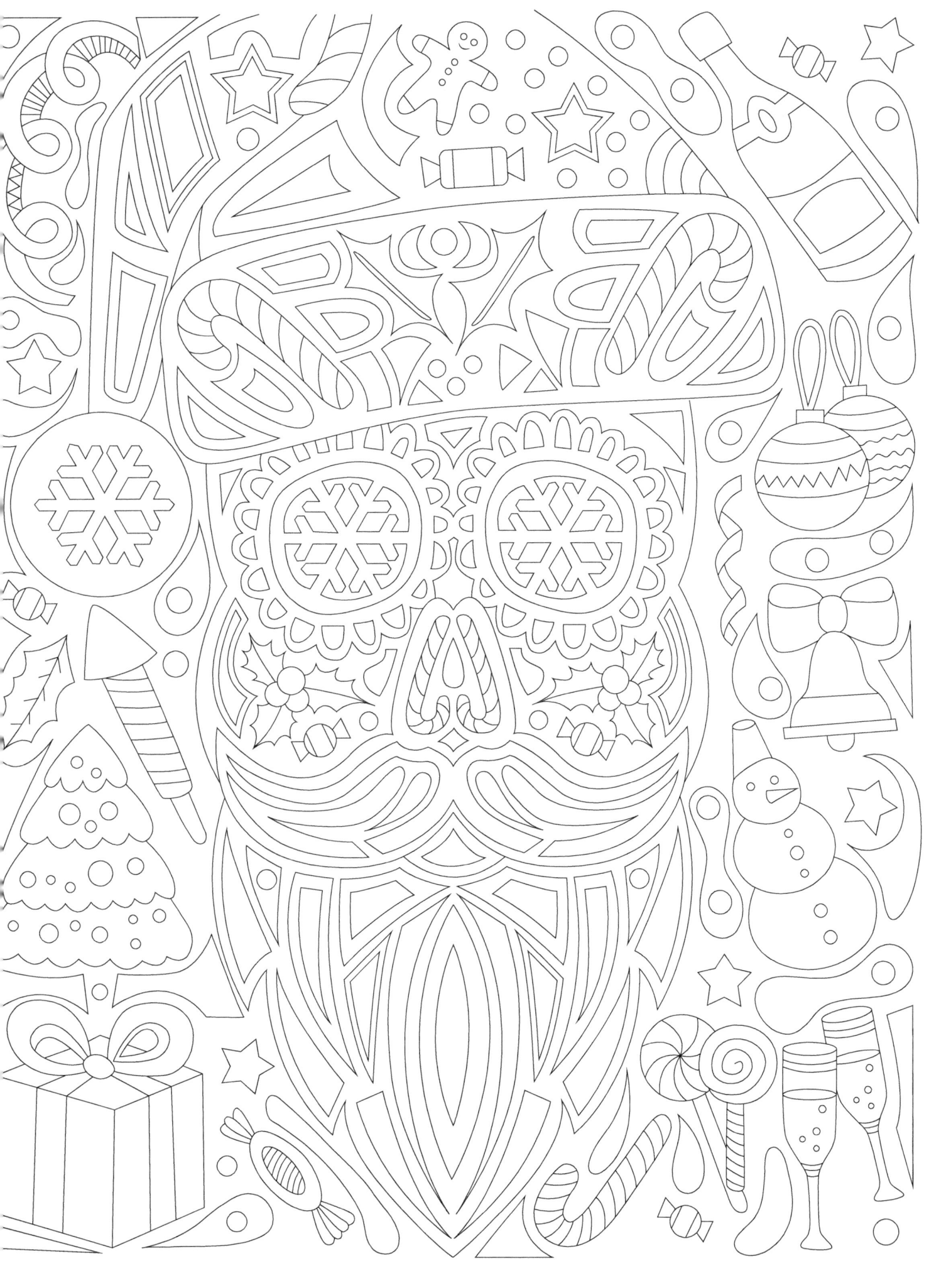

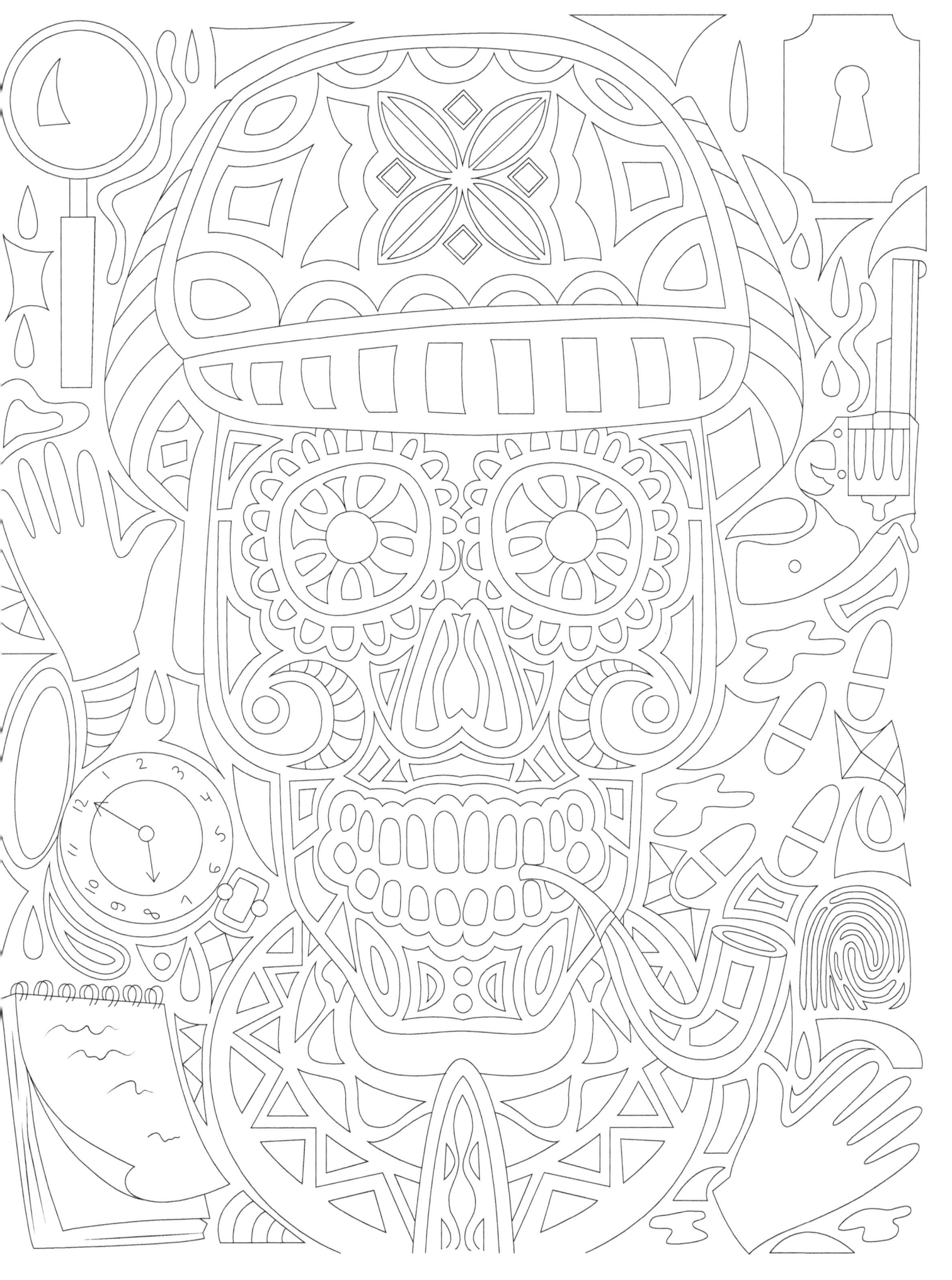

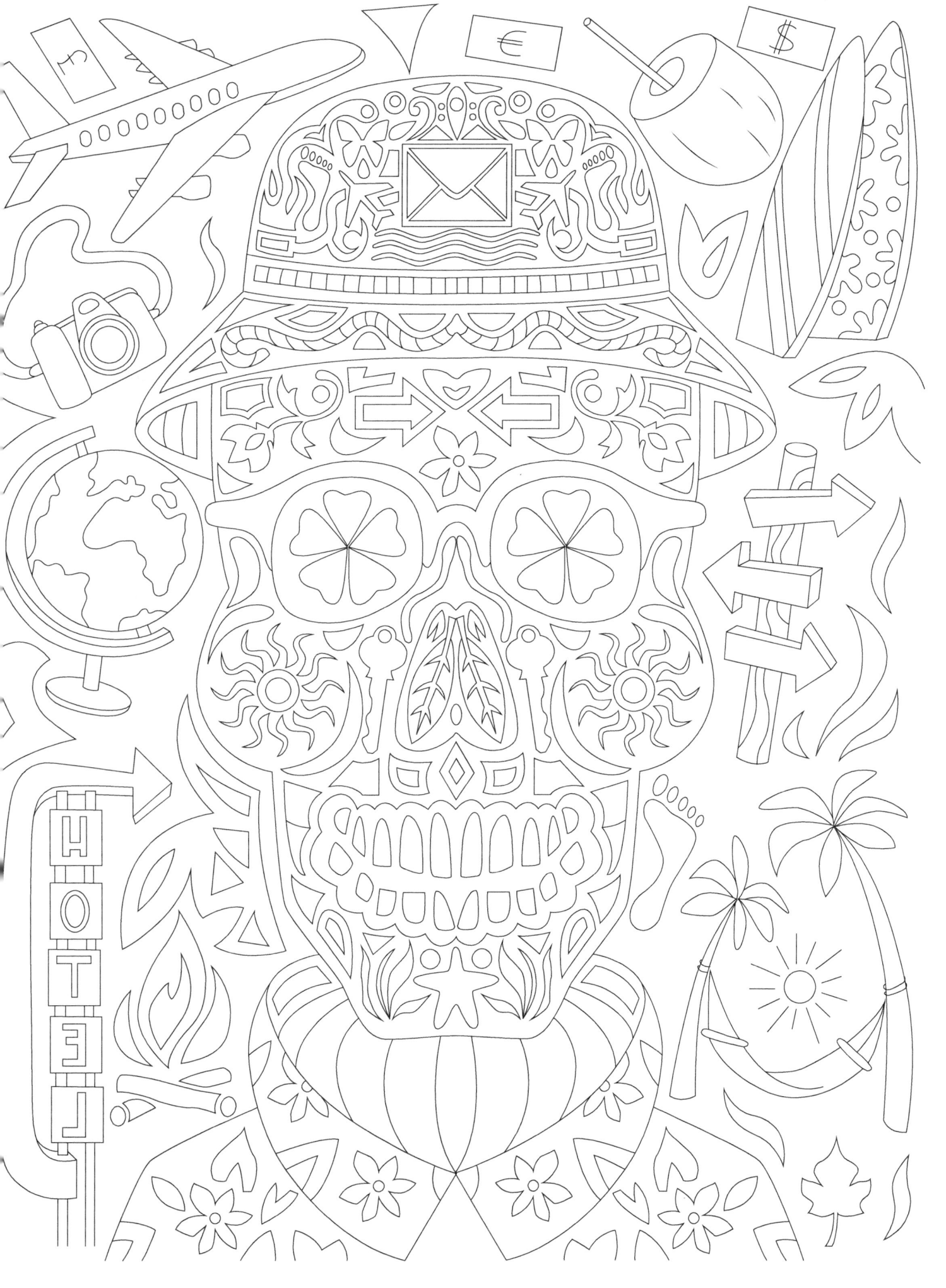

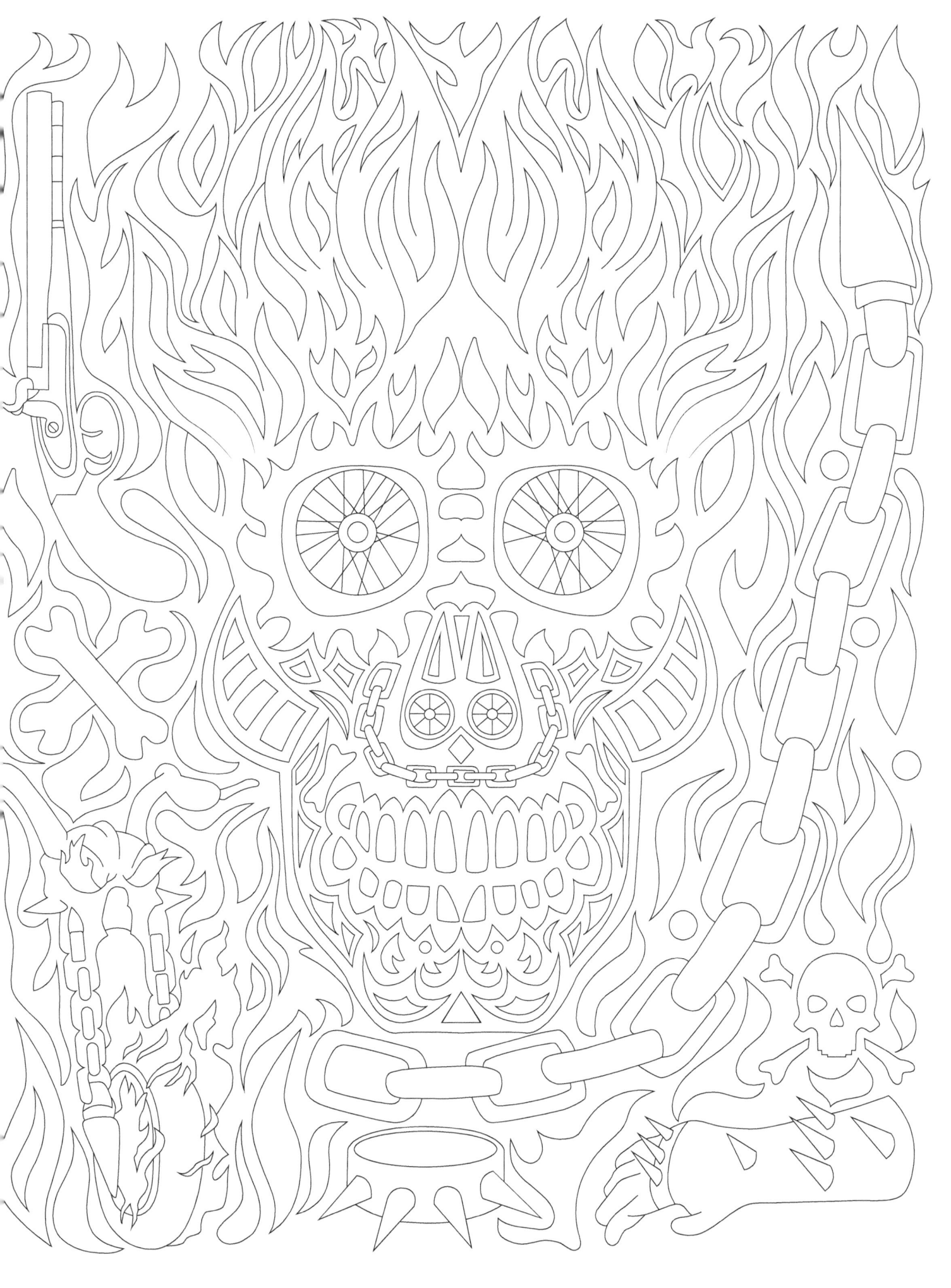

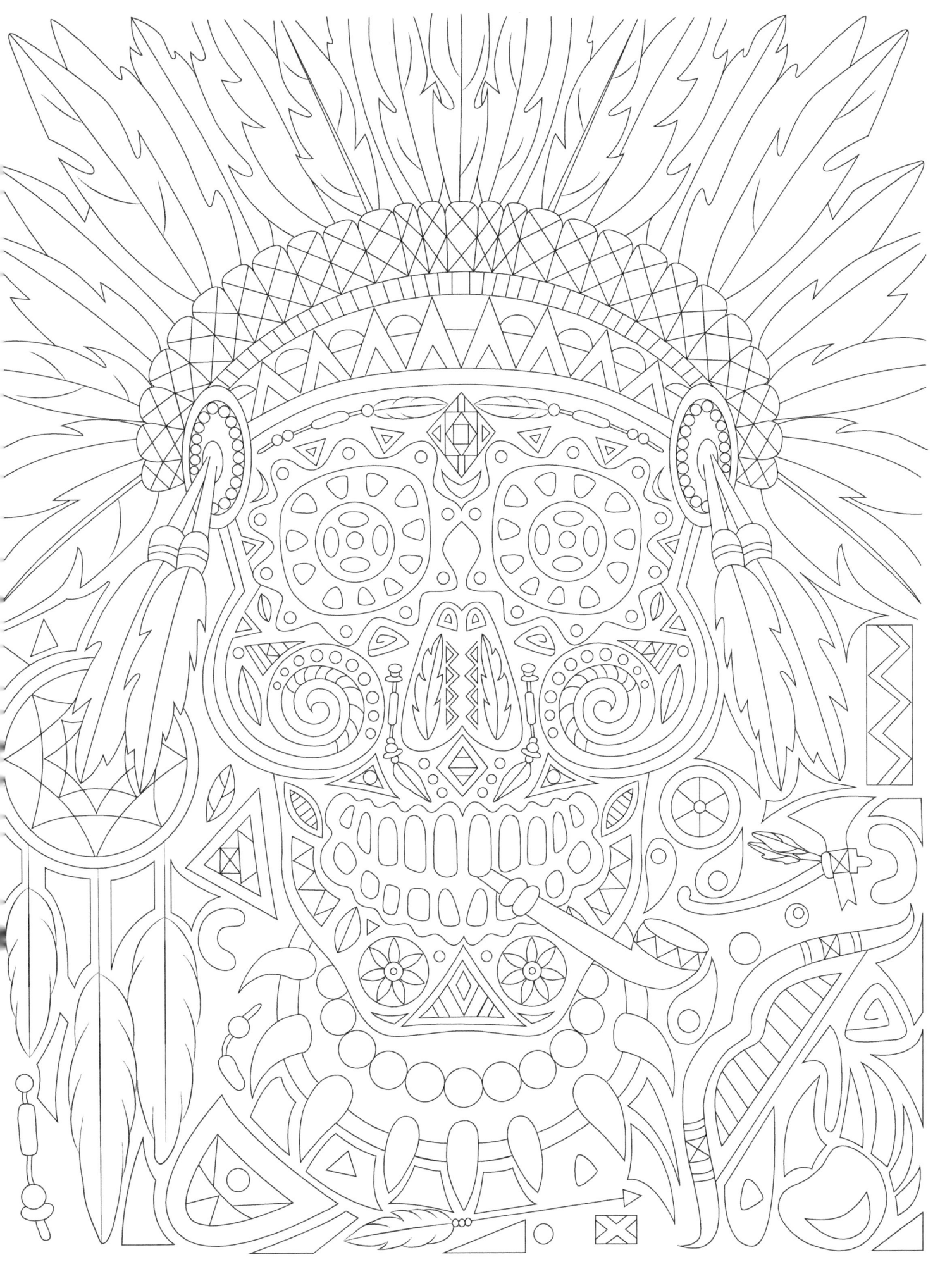

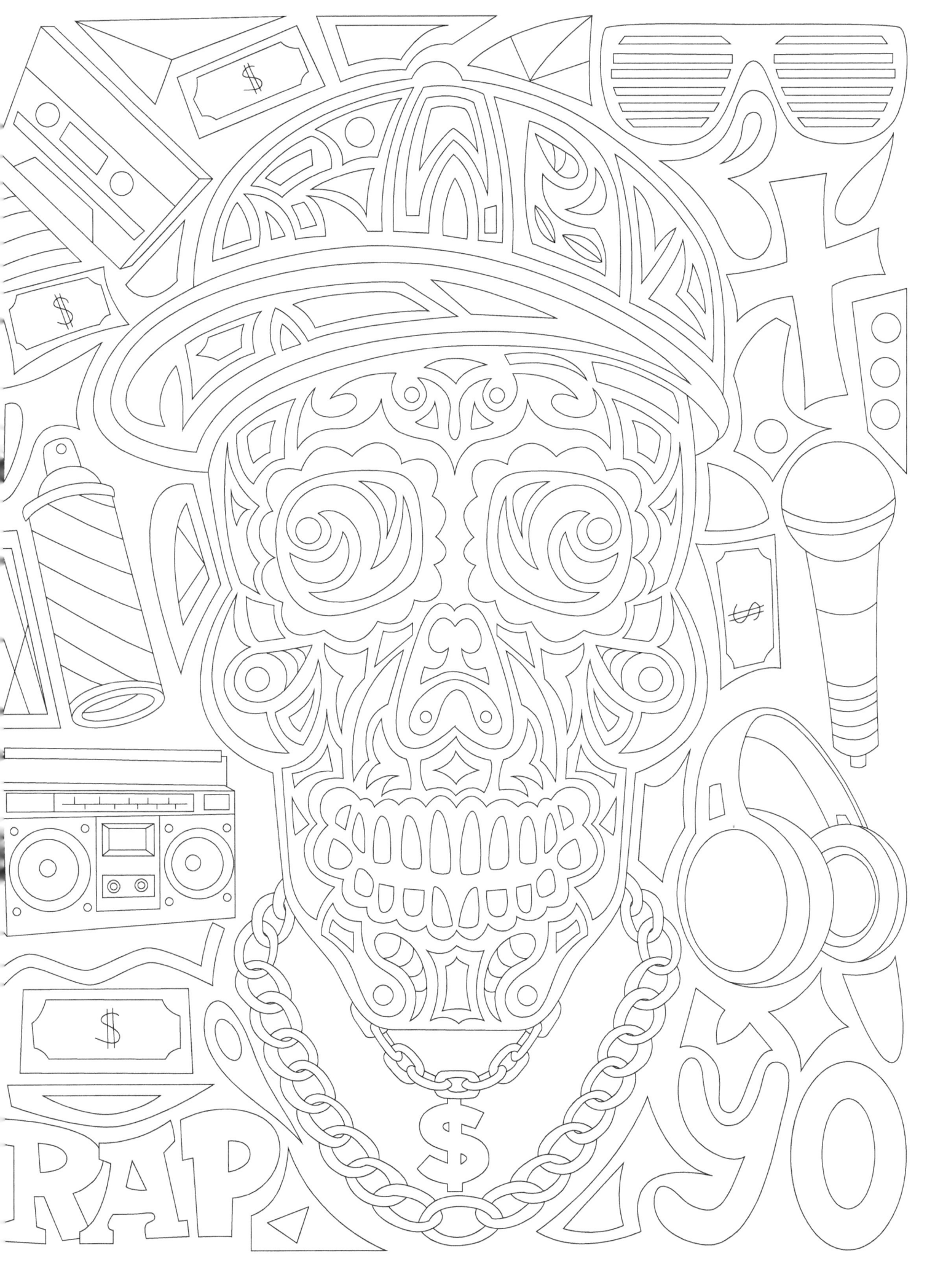

TRY OUR QUEST COLOR BY NUMBER BOOKS

THANK YOU for choosing our book, we hope you **LIKED IT**. Fill free to write **YOUR REVIEW** and share **YOUR ART-WORKS** on **AMAZON**. We want to know **YOUR IMPRESSION** of the book.

And we want to **PRESENT YOU** pages from our **QUEST COLOR BY NUMBER** books:

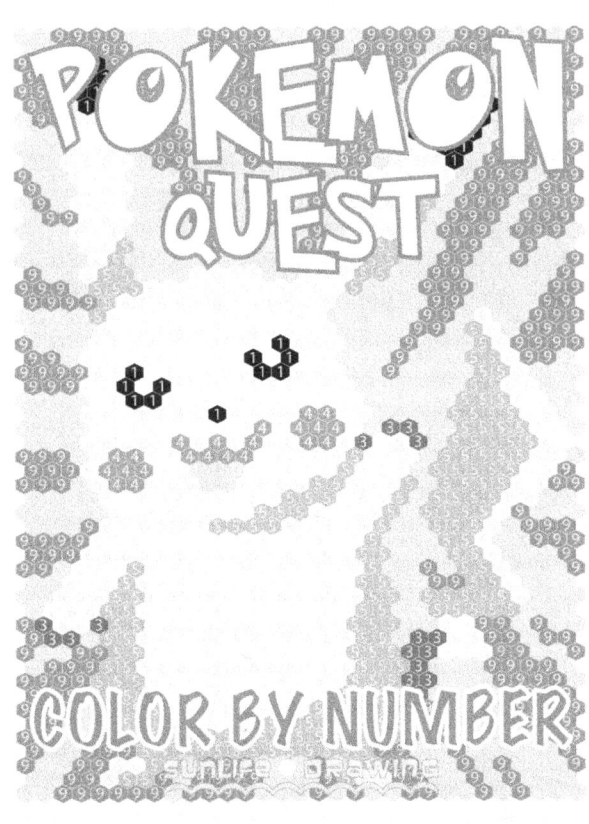

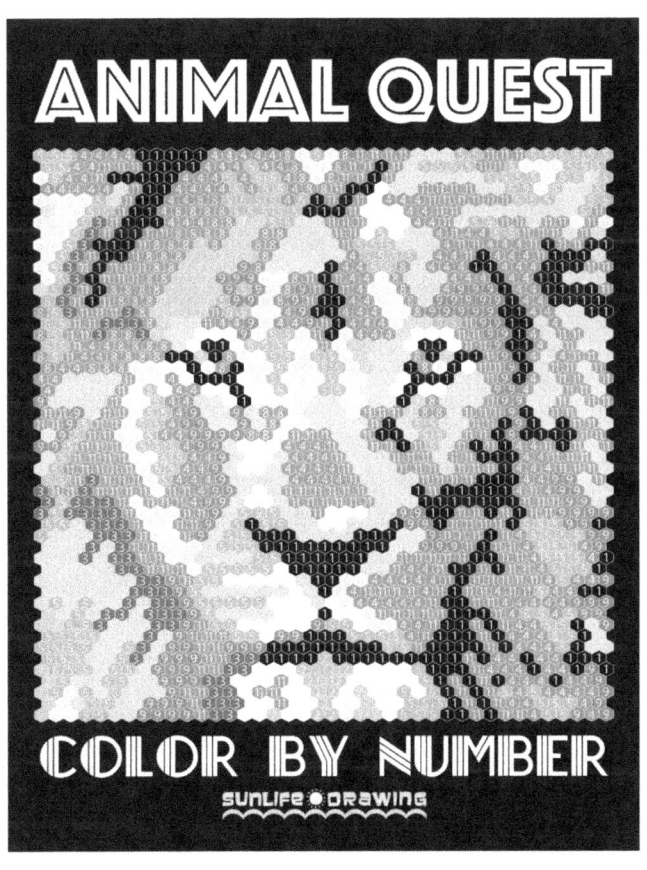

FULL versions of these books you can **BUY** on **AMAZON.**

1	BLACK	
2	GRAY	
3	BROWN	
4	RED	
5	ORANGE	
6	YELLOW	
7	LIGHT GREEN	
8	GREEN	
9	BLUE	
10	SKY BLUE	
11	PURPLE	
12	PINK